W9-CKI-607

CHEROKEE

Big Buddy Books
An Imprint of Abdo Publishing
www.abdopublishing.com

Sarah Tieck

www.abdopublishing.com

Published by Abdo Publishing, a division of ABDO, PO Box 398166, Minneapolis, Minnesota 55439.
Copyright © 2015 by Abdo Consulting Group, Inc. International copyrights reserved in all countries. No part
of this book may be reproduced in any form without written permission from the publisher. Big Buddy Books™
is a trademark and logo of Abdo Publishing.

Printed in the United States of America, North Mankato, Minnesota.
052014
092014

Cover Photo: ASSOCIATED PRESS.
Interior Photos: © Danita Delimont/Alamy (p. 21); Getty Images (p. 30); © Buddy Mays/Alamy (p. 15);
   © NativeStock.com/AngelWynn (pp. 5, 9, 16, 17, 19, 25); © North Wind/Nancy Carter/North Wind Picture
   Archives (p. 27); © North Wind/North Wind Picture Archives (pp. 21, 26); © Luc Novovitch/Alamy (pp. 13, 17);
   Print Collector/Getty Images (p. 23); Shutterstock (pp. 11, 17); UIG via Getty Images (p. 29).

Coordinating Series Editor: Rochelle Baltzer
Contributing Editors: Bridget O'Brien, Marcia Zappa
Graphic Design: Adam Craven

Library of Congress Cataloging-in-Publication Data

Tieck, Sarah, 1976-
  Cherokee / Sarah Tieck.
      pages cm. -- (Native Americans)
  ISBN 978-1-62403-352-0
1. Cherokee Indians--History--Juvenile literature. 2. Cherokee Indians--Social life and customs--Juvenile literature.
I. Title.
  E99.C5T54 2014
  975.004'97557--dc23
                            2014006316

CONTENTS

AMAZING PEOPLE

Hundreds of years ago, North America was mostly wild, open land. Native Americans lived there. They had their own languages and customs.

The Cherokee (CHEHR-uh-kee) are a Native American nation. They are known for their powerful women and their writing system. Let's learn more about these Native Americans.

Did You Know?

The name *Cherokee* means "people of different speech." This came from a Creek Native American word. The Cherokee called themselves *Ani'-Yun'wiya* or *Tsalagi*.

Modern Cherokee often dress in traditional clothes for ceremonies.

CHEROKEE TERRITORY

The Cherokee are a large nation of people. Their homelands were in the southeastern United States. They lived in parts of present-day Georgia, Alabama, Tennessee, Kentucky, West Virginia, Virginia, North Carolina, and South Carolina. Their land was in the Appalachian Mountains.

CANADA

UNITED STATES

CHEROKEE HOMELANDS

WEST
VIRGINIA

VIRGINIA

KENTUCKY

NORTH CAROLINA

TENNESSEE

SOUTH
CAROLINA

MISSISSIPPI

GEORGIA

ALABAMA

N
W E
S

MEXICO

7

Home Life

The Cherokee lived in wattle and daub houses. These homes were made for just one family.

The house frame was built from river cane, wood, and vines. It was coated with clay. The clay that covered the frame dried very hard. This took time, but made a strong house. The roof was made of grass or bark. There were no windows.

Did You Know?

By the late 1700s, many Cherokee lived in log cabins.

The Cherokee built smaller homes for the winter. These had roofs made of wood and clay like the rest of the home. This helped the people stay warm.

What They Ate

The Cherokee were hunters, gatherers, and farmers. The men hunted animals such as deer and turkeys. They also fished. The tribe gathered wild berries. The women farmed corn, beans, and squash. They turned these into meals including stew and corn bread.

Turkeys were a good food source for the Cherokee. Males can weigh up to 22 pounds (10 kg).

Daily Life

A Cherokee village had 30 to 60 homes. Each family had their own home for living and sleeping. They built fires for cooking and warmth. People made tools, clothes, and other important objects.

Until the early 1800s, the Cherokee wore clothes made from animal skin. Later, they began wearing European clothing. This included jackets and head coverings. Women wore dresses.

 Deer hide leggings helped protect the legs from plant scratches.

In each village, people had different jobs. Men hunted, fished, and trapped. Cherokee men were strong fighters and tribe chiefs. Being powerful was important to them. Sometimes, they played a game called stickball. It helped them settle fights without going to war.

Women were very important. In most places, people organize society based on the father's family. But, Cherokee clans were organized based on the mother's family. Also, women served in the tribe's government.

Did You Know?

The Cherokee became known for their strong, organized government system.

In 1985, Wilma Mankiller became the first female principal chief of the Cherokee. She worked to make life better for Cherokee people.

15

Made by Hand

The Cherokee made many objects by hand. They used materials from nature. These arts and crafts added beauty to their lives. They were also useful.

Handmade Baskets

Cherokee women made double-wall baskets from grasses. A double-wall basket has an inside wall and outside wall woven together. Some baskets had colorful patterns. They had many uses, such as holding food.

River Cane Objects

River cane grows near creek banks and swamps. The Cherokee used the stems to make blowguns and flutes. They painted the river cane, so the objects were pretty.

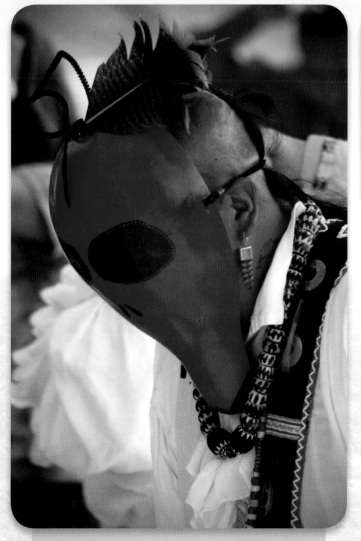

Masks

The Cherokee made masks from wood or gourds. Many were meant to be ugly and odd looking to keep away bad forces. They wore them during a special dance called "the Booger Dance."

Clay Pottery

The Cherokee made pottery. They dug up clay from the earth. They made it into cooking pots, bowls, water jugs, and other items. Then they marked the clay using tools, such as stamping paddles.

Spirit Life

Religion was important to the Cherokee. The tribe believed in order and balance. They had six special ceremonies every year. Others happened during the year, too.

At these ceremonies, the men and women would eat certain foods and dance in circles. They might include fire or sacred objects as part of a ceremony.

Did You Know?

The numbers seven and four are important to the Cherokee. Special colors include red, blue, black, and white.

Dancing is part of Cherokee ceremonies and festivals.

STORYTELLERS

The Cherokee were famous for their written language. It was invented in the early 1800s by a Cherokee man named Sequoyah.

Before that, the Cherokee had no written words. So, they told stories to teach people about their history. They also shared ideas about how their people fit into the world. Even after they had written words, storytelling remained important.

  Sequoyah became famous for starting the Cherokee written language.

  Sometimes the Cherokee played music or wore masks to tell stories.

FIGHTING FOR LAND

In the 1540s, Europeans first arrived on Cherokee land. Later, they settled the area. Many Cherokee died from sicknesses they caught from them.

The Cherokee attacked settlers to **protect** their homelands. Nanye'hi, or Nancy Ward, was a Beloved Woman. Around 1785, she began using her power to help bring peace. She worked with the US government for many years.

Did You Know?

A Beloved Woman was an important female leader in a Cherokee tribe.

 The Cherokee fought European
settings to keep control of their land.

In 1829, gold was found on Cherokee land. American settlers wanted the land. In 1830, the Indian Removal Act became a law. It said all Native Americans had to move west of the Mississippi River.

Some Cherokee agreed to move. But many wanted to stay. In 1838, the US Army forced the Cherokee and other tribes to leave. The tribes walked or rode horses about 800 miles (1,300 km) to land west of the Mississippi River. This was called the Trail of Tears.

Today, many Cherokee live in northeast Oklahoma, North Carolina, and Tennessee. They work to protect their land and way of life.

 On the Trail of Tears, many Native Americans became sick. Thousands died.

BACK IN TIME

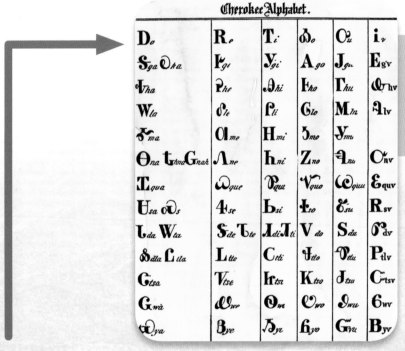

Cherokee Alphabet.

1821

The Cherokee began using Sequoyah's written language. This made it possible for them to start schools and print newspapers.

1700s

The Cherokee caught sicknesses, such as smallpox, from European settlers. Many died.

1827

The Cherokee made their first constitution.

Around 1870

The Eastern Band of Cherokee established their government in North Carolina.

1976

The Cherokee Nation government was started again. It had been taken apart in 1906.

"TRAIL OF TEARS"

AFTER CONGRESS PASSED THE INDIAN REMOVAL ACT, MAY 28, 1830, THE GOVERNMENT FORCEABLY RELOCATED ABOUT 60,000 INDIANS FROM THE SOUTHEASTERN U.S. TO WHAT IS NOW OKLAHOMA. THIS INCLUDED THE FIVE (5) CIVILIZED TRIBES: CHEROKEE, CHICKASAW, CREEK, CHOCTAW, AND SEMINOLE.

WHEN ANDREW JACKSON RAN FOR PRESIDENT IN 1829, HE PLEDGED TO MOVE THE INDIANS WEST OF THE MISSISSIPPI RIVER. AFTER REMOVAL BECAME LAW, THE GOVERNMENT PROCEEDED TO RELOCATE THE INDIANS. SOME TRAVELLED OVERLAND AND OTHERS BY WATER. MANY SUFFERED SEVERE HARDSHIPS.

ABOUT 14,000 CHEROKEE WERE RELOCATED WITH 4,000 DEATHS OCCURING. THE GRIEF FROM THEIR LOVED ONES' DEATHS, THE HARDSHIPS AND DEPRIVATIONS, MADE THEIR TREK WESTWARD INDEED A "TRAIL OF TEARS".

ERECTED BY CONWAY CHAMBER OF COMMERCE
FAULKNER COUNTY HISTORICAL SOCIETY
IN COOPERATION WITH U.S. ARMY CORPS OF ENGINEERS
OCTOBER, 1989

1838

Thousands of Cherokee walked about 800 miles (1,300 km) in what is called the Trail of Tears. Later, memorials were built to honor the lives lost.

A Strong Nation

The Cherokee people have a long, rich history. They are remembered for their powerful women and strong government. They are also known for their beautiful baskets and written language.

Cherokee roots run deep. Today, the people have kept alive those special things that make them Cherokee. Even though times have changed, many people carry the traditions, stories, and memories of the past into the present.

Did You Know?

Today, there are about 285,000 Cherokee living in the United States. They are one of the country's largest Native American nations.

The Cherokee hold powwows. They dance, sing, and honor traditions at these gatherings.

"Cherokee traditional identity is tied to both an individual and collective determination to follow a good path, be responsible and loving, and help one another – or as some Cherokee traditionalists say, 'Not let go of one another.'"

— Wilma Mankiller

GLOSSARY

ceremony a formal event on a special occasion.

constitution (kahnt-stuh-TOO-shuhn) the basic laws that govern a nation or a state.

custom a practice that has been around a long time and is common to a group or a place.

protect (pruh-TEHKT) to guard against harm or danger.

sacred (SAY-kruhd) connected with worship of a god.

smallpox a sickness that causes fever, skin marks, and often death.

tradition (truh-DIH-shuhn) a belief, a custom, or a story handed down from older people to younger people.

WEBSITES

To learn more about Native Americans, visit **booklinks.abdopublishing.com**. These links are routinely monitored and updated to provide the most current information available.

INDEX